Quilcene

Avis M. Adams

Finishing Line Press
Georgetown, Kentucky

Quilcene

Copyright © 2019 by Avis M. Adams
ISBN 978-1-63534-920-7 First Edition
All rights reserved under International and Pan-American Copyright Conventions. No part of this book may be reproduced in any manner whatsoever without written permission from the publisher, except in the case of brief quotations embodied in critical articles and reviews.

ACKNOWLEDGMENTS

I would like to thank Deborah Woodard for her friendship and constant support in all things, especially poetry Marjorie Rommel for her inspiration. Trevor O'Hara for his keen eye and ability in the craft. And last but not least, the Black Diamond Crew, Ardi, Harvey, Suzanne, and Skeeter, who always let me know when something is working and when it isn't. My poetry is better for their valuable critiques.

Publisher: Leah Maines
Editor: Christen Kincaid
Cover Art: Avis Adams
Author Photo: Michael F. Adams
Cover Design: Leah Huete

Printed in the USA on acid-free paper.
Order online: www.finishinglinepress.com
also available on amazon.com

Author inquiries and mail orders:
Finishing Line Press
P. O. Box 1626
Georgetown, Kentucky 40324
U. S. A.

Table of Contents

Cellophane 1

Successful Dogs 2

Clothesline 4

Japanese Garden 6

Green Jeans 7

Preparing for the Funeral 9

Quilcene 10

Gracefully Nude 11

Bibliothéque 13

Autumn 16

Serpentina 17

A Haunting at Edgefield 18

Ruston Way 21

Bearded Iris 23

Truth and Beauty 24

Dimensions 26

Honed 27

August 28

The Precious Names 29

Wild Thoughts 30

Golden Maple 31

Hara 32

*Dedicated to the people I love.
You know who you are.*

Cellophane

We'd look first for snow
then listen for closures
of schools and roads.

We'd slip on two pairs
of white socks, stained
gray at heel and toe,

and a cellophane bag
for each booted foot.
We'd play in a frozen
forest of fir and moss

until the snow
began to melt
and the slush

would steal
through leaky soles.

Successful Dogs

We are, we always were,
successful dogs.
Until I fell one day, as a rock
from the rapture, and landed

in this tall, thin town
of cinder block houses
and shared telephones.
I would send you a message,

but how do I reach your high-rise
manners now? My eyes linger
on the brilliant light
cast like reverse shadow.

It radiates desperate exchanges,
exposes a bristle of cracks
and spidery veins to leak
our secrets into the air.

The stars resemble
bullets of chalk—
white larvae, my
unraveling life.

They sing my song
as naked trees with dancing
limbs barely conceal windows.
I imagine sending you a visitor,

receiving a pardon,
but, oh, the visitation,
the hot bullets I would broadcast.
Figures of crab and spectacle bear

scintillate into the fallen light,
remind me of my time
on the calendar and
the windows I opened

to this dim vocation.

Clotheslines

I ask him to hang a line between two
trees, or deck standards, where I can
sunburn sheets and recreate the dark smell
hidden under covers, the coarse fibers

a relief to skin overexposed to sun
and untamed words.
Traffic sounds are muffled through inner-
city clotheslines. Among the panty

hose, pair after pair, hang flannel gowns
and cotton boxers. They flap in ghostly
shapes, frail and without form, collapsed
and wrinkled. Dresses and slacks sag

like branches as frozen air sucks moisture
from cloth. It chills the warm body brittle.
I watch until we drive around a curve
of Highway 99.

At Pier 1, the label reads,
"tranquility for the bath." I
pry the lid, inhale my grandmother's
closet on a midsummer day.

The open window lifts cream sheers.
The dairy cattle low, swaying
to the barn between tongue pulls
of sweet grass.

Clothes hang from wooden pins, each
nylon stocking a separate shell for my
grandmother's legs, my red pants
wrinkled next to her polka-dot shirt.

And the deck railing becomes an impromptu
clothesline, where little boy's briefs
hang by bigger men's briefs. They dry
in folds over the wood. The smaller

briefs drift to the ivy below, become a home
to spiders and centipedes. The occasional
pine needle hinges stiffness in a sock.
It mimics the stiffness of your cool lips

pressed on mine.

Japanese Garden

Suspended on air,
skippers prick the pond's
surface with four toes.

Scattered by a shadow,
they glide, first one
then two then six.

Under the reflections
of western hemlock
and stands of bamboo,

a school of koi,
orange and fleshy,
follow the leader

amidst tail flicks.
Sand rises in agitated tufts
to settle in ridges.

Green Jeans

Black cowboy boots
tucked into green jeans
loose at the knees, my shirt
snapped with pearl buttons. The
ski jacket came after I'd
learned the humiliation of giggles
rippling down the hall, eyes following
me in pairs

and quartets. Those social
neophytes looked me down
then up, never reaching
my eyes. My mother's sale
shopping at Wigwam haunted
my initiation into miniskirts
and go-go boots I
would never own.

My first shoplift at Sally's
on Main Street was an orange
angora sweater that my
youngest sister threw into the dryer.
I wore it once after that, my
exposed navel another faux pas
in my recurring social failures.

Except when my favorite
grandfather died and Mom paid
full price for the bell-bottom
jeans and flour sack top. I felt
beautiful then. I could walk
down hallways an immediate
member, recognizable as not
the horse-crazy girl.

I burned those jeans,
and my third sister,
the recipient of my hand-me-downs,
smiled her buck-toothed smile
and lisped her thanks.
I danced with my friends
to Three Dog Night
and Zeppelin,
the memory of green jeans
only a dull film to replay
before my next period.

Preparing for the Funeral

On the bench, a hammer waited for his gnarled
fingers. He'd pound in nails to his favorite tunes of swing
and pop.

Rubber galoshes skidded to the barn, bruised
the grass. The window framed Dad tinkering
with hinges from the door. He spun familiar
talk, his jaw a common bone we shared.

The call came too late; his relic detoured
to dance in our front room. Dad lit the air,
swayed like a constellation, a fragment
of the Milky Way. I worried the house
with silent bellows.

Sun filtered through dirty glass to lay
silent on the hardwood floor in angular
maps.

I knew him better for that airy jig.
His explanation of black, bunched eyebrows
over eyes that had seen World War II,
water stains on the ceiling, and holes
in his daughter's socks.

From Arizona, California,
Idaho, Montana they came. I
loaned them pillows, fed them. Dad rambled
among us, brushing a cheek, riding
a chuckle. His best profile was called
upon.

The bouquet on the piano dripped petals.
Its scent, like overripe fruit, oiled
the musty air.

Quilcene

a blue-sky day mottled by clouds
so white their edges cut the eye

from the southeast a gyrating mist
under a layer of billowed iron

that rushes
a dispersed atmosphere

an uneven blending of white cotton
over gray wool then black dots

birds
a seagull, two wrens, a crow

they crease the pattern
a seam of wings

beating against the flow of Dvorak

Gracefully Nude

Tinted in shades of sepia, the Cascade
foothills lay behind a brown malaise
that enters lungs on the inhale,
is not exhaled. Clouds rush to embrace

Mount Rainier, a movement her husband
once made toward her. The clouds
loose an abundance of spatters, wet and
large. They married on such a day. The

slanted rain as it leapt off the asphalt
seemed jolly, and the dark kitten that
also leapt about in a frenzy on the wet
asphalt became symbolic of his response.

Don't look. It didn't happen.
She waited for his words to change,
to become expressions of comfort.
In her emptiness, she waited

for these words, yet he remained
sullen, quiet. She created a narrative
and dreamed his voice in the dialog.
It sufficed, until the day a question

was asked and in her narrative
she could not find the answer.
As she rummaged through words
that had never existed, she fell

instead into the vacuum of her desires.
When she woke, a man was speaking,
and she cried to hear his words. She
wanted them to be sacred, yet they

could not craft the language she yearned
for. They, too, hung in absented warmth.
She wrote them down and smiled to see
her own ciphers, the space captured by

each letter. Her husband seeks her now
for his physical articulations,
and she learns to listen to
his touch. Steel gray suffuses their landscape,

yet green memories linger in red-tipped branches,
gracefully nude, their fingers reaching.

Bibliothéque

I.

In October, the sky is blue. Fingers stroke
the crystal knob, and slowly, the door gaps.
My child's body glides into the sanctuary,

the aviary, where flocks of titles congregate,
propagate, lead my eyes north and south.
Fingers graze the middle shelf, read the leather

bindings. An oak desk squats stubbornly
in the center of the room. The southern
exposure warms the books, perfumes my hair,

anoints my body—sweet wood, thick air,
slow time. *Dr Zhivago* beckons. A patch
of rainbow lies on the desk. I read until Yury's

firm hand seems to clutch my shoulder
and my friend pulls me back to sunshine
and childhood and laughter.

II.

From girl to woman rocking, pregnant
with language—French, Spanish, Dickens,
Cervantes, Chopin. My son is delivered

between Flaubert and Dickinson. The
bentwood rocker creaks back and forth—
rock and read. The cane seat forms to my

seat. I rock to the tick of the clock.
The cuckoo perched at two as I read and rock.

III.

The dream comes, rows and stacks of books,
their names calling to me—*The Man from La Manche,
Great Expectations.* I wander in their geography,

my child at my breast, while I suckle words
from the page. I feed on landscapes of Spain
and the rain on Market Street in Londonderry,

ride the coach to Bath, all to escape the truth
of a benefactor—whom I realize I need—
and tighten my hold on my child. He stirs,

a flow of milk escaping over lips and tongue.
My eyes lick the page for windmills and lances
and rusty armor. Whose Dulcinea am I, weighted

to this rocker, new life in my arms? I dream
of walking into a warm, book-filled room
and breathing the aroma of old lace too long

by the fire. The rocker moans to the ticking
of the clock, my child's heartbeat next to mine.
I turn the page.

IV.

Air filters through leaded glass as the mumbled
echoes of words fill the room. Vaulted ribs
straddle my thoughts like rows of legs. I open

the dictionary, inspire the dust to a sneeze
that echoes in the graduate reading room.
Ready to inhale the fumes of G: gerontology,

gentian, gesundheit, goulashes. Backward to E:
equality, equestrian, equine, equinox. Words
that unhinge knowledge, memory. My eyes fill

with characters. Abstractions crowd my brain.
Suckling words from bound pages,
I read.

Autumn

Orange and yellow
paint the trees
like bright flames
on Montlake Boulevard,
like a tapestry I
once saw of sunflowers
in South Dakota.
I trace the pattern
onto fabric,
the colorless outline.
I collect thread
of Hooker's green
and amber,
of yellow ochre,
burnt umber,
and silver.
The threads stitch
a scene of trees,
the Black Hills
in autumn.
The loose ends
hide Father.
He hangs
behind the landscape
of leaves and bark.
He hikes the tangled
wilderness of paths
that cut through bur oak
and yellow pine
to trout filled streams.

Serpentina

The sun in its blue sky haunted August fence posts,
traced the cracks along the south tower.
The shadows at noon whitewashed
yet stained by the insignificance of a twig,
I stood alert, preparing for flight from the serpent.
I expected him to come bearing olive

branches, but I would relish the olives,
even if I had to walk the rows of posts,
eyes searching for the ever-present serpent.
Once I dreamed of escaping to the tower.
I ached for dreams that broke like twigs,
abandoned in the corner of my heart, whitewashed.

It never occurred to me that whitewash
limed the skin, clogged pores of olive,
and bristled hairs along the arm, a twig.
The real test came with barbed wire. Posts
held fast in earth, the wire strung from tower
to tower. Grass grew in clumps that concealed serpents.

The olive orchard attracted children like serpents
to the original garden, our innocence a whitewash
of dirt under our nails. We towered
over the younger children, pits to our olives.
They followed us until we shimmied the post,
and they, in ripe gladness, rustled like twigs.

A Haunting at Edgefield

I.

The bagpipes blow every year on New Year's
Eve to dispel the airy confusion.
Every year, the idea of decades replays

on each note, and every year, the work farm
residents, the nursing home residents,
the artists all remember the first day

they came to this redbrick place with curiosity
and ran their fingers along the stairwell wall.

II.

Torn yellow wallpaper, a small piece
hanging from the wall in the room
where we will sleep.

That's when I see her by the pay
phone, a woman, elderly. She smiles
as she stands tangled in the pattern

of torn yellow wall paper, a floral dragon
repeated for some reason. Her bemused
smile begs for answers, now.

III.

The first black rabbit fills the canvas,
a conspicuous Harvey in recovery.
The second and third rabbits creep into corners

of larger landscapes, of farm workers harvesting
carrots and mowing hay. The fourth
black rabbit, a proud steed,

carries Mr. Toad. The fifth
sits in a field by a white
cottage, looking at the artist, no sepia tone
to subdue the glossy, black coat.

IV.

The haunting seems to regress on cloudy
nights. Thin plywood doors clamor in the cool
air. Three times the clatter comes. And the dull

thud of trying, of vibration, a vacuum
sucking. It stirs the solitude.
The door rattles, shakes the panes

in wooden frames while tendrils
of paint thread through old dreams that fell
away to newer ideas and different needs,

wider doors for hospital beds and chairs
on wheels. The glue of people, the essence
of their lives, connected through the geography

of this place, connected now through the oil-
based hues on walls and doors.

V.

Thirteen bagpipes execute "Amazing
Grace," prying loose the hold
of Satan and various poltergeists

that populate certain rooms
and haunt certain portals.
The melody stirs echoes

off the paint on ceilings and
stairwells. It reawakens the twinkle
in the eye of an aging Venus, on the smiles

of octogenarian nymphs climbing
the water tower as the bagpipes
moan and calm replaces discord.

Ruston Way

Short days bring us
to Ruston Way for walks in the rain.
Shaman runs over clipped
grass. She drags a red leash

as we climb down the shallow
bank to lolling water.
I listen to you speak,
watch your eyes,

the wrinkles in your forehead
and then look to the Cascades,
your words strung on the waves,
rolling with the pebbles.

Across Commencement Bay,
the mountains hunker
under gray clouds,
blue slopes cloaked in snow.

You speak of a woman
as double-crested cormorants
bob and sway on the cold, green
water, dive to catch

fish. A heron
hunkers blue shoulders
and swings over water
to the next barnacle-
shrouded boulder.
We follow, and the heron
veers in the opposite direction.

Pilings lurch from a sandy beach,
and gulls perch, watching us.
Still you speak a circular logic
that folds in on itself,

never completing the ring.
Another heron preens,
beak running through back feathers,
the long, stiff wing feathers.

The scent of saltwater lingers,
a whisper on the breeze.
Brick foundations exposed
by water are overlaid in places

with sod and asphalt. I listen
to you sigh as pieces and parcels
of red clay lie broken yet smooth
cornered on the beach. They lend

their carnival color to the gray
sand and motley pebbles
that fill our sight.

Bearded Iris

> *... and then the day came when the risk to remain tight in a bud was more painful than the risk it took to blossom.* ~Anais Nin

Tightly packed buds rise
on slender stalks
under your bedroom window.
You watch the flower heads

each cool spring day.
Warmer days loosen their hold
on purple. Condensed
in a crepe-like seal,
they unpack themselves.

The buds swell beyond
the transparent protection,
beyond the bruised flesh
of awkward youth.

One morning, you wake
to the blue sky competing
with a flock of iris,
and you see your father's

shoulders
there in the iris bed,
bent to the ground,
planting.

Truth and Beauty

The photographer of your first-
grade class called you Sweetie.
At ten years of age, I dispised you.

Those quiet overcast days spent
indoors while condensation
bled down the windows
and potatoes boiled every

evening at precisely five.
I felt it envelop me, the smell
of creamed tuna and harsh words
and the loud cries for Mommy or Daddy.

What did they mean, those words?
You said once that Mom
got the beauty, left nothing
for you.

I was the oldest,
could not do the math
that you made look easy.
It floated through my mind,
never settling. Yet you never

understood the meaning of *disastrous*
until you asked me for a word
to describe Mom's new hairdo.
I blamed you for the loud silence

that filled the space where Dad should
have stood but didn't. I blamed you
for the whiskey bottles that clanked
under the seat of his station

wagon. You, the selfish one.
The woman who would bear children
but not their fathers. You, who lived
in solitude, went on the prowl.

Now you struggle between the freedom
you inhale
and the slow death of comfortable shoes.

Dimensions

The steep ascent was nothing.
It was the looking
that hurt—for snakes.

I found birds.
He once read to me
in an aviary.

I was the bird he would not cage
while I perched on the ledge
of his knowledge,

on the gyration of his words.

No arms can hold you,
he said, yet I wanted
to hold him forever.

An osprey rose from her
nest, described an arc
in three dimensions.

I watched her cut over the valley
as I scaled the ridge,
understanding well my marriage

to gravity.

Honed

by cancer,
she sits at the bistro table,
thin but strong,

wise in ways
that are unknown
to me.

She battles the dragon,
and I realize
the magnitude of my denial.

I look at her and see
the purple and red scarf
under her black hat.

I see her jeans,
loose in the thigh,
and her slender hands

that balance a cup
of tea, and I see
her fragile smile.

As we talk, I witness
her black eyes
shine with a light born

of keen understanding.
Cancer has taken a part of her,
yet she remains,

victorious.

August

Lethargic in their flight,
June bugs hover,
the August heat dripping.

Dust gilds the salal
and Oregon grape
along our driveway.

These days push us
over the edge of our
conscious desire.

Long stemmed grasses,
green in July,
bend to the ground,

a golden mat in August,
as the seed heads
spill their fruit,

the subtle languor
of this bend to earth
a sensual arc.

Who am I to write
such things—the heat in August,
the dust on leaves, the falling fruit?

After splendid fertility,
I bend to the earth now,
a shadow on the harvest.

The Precious Names

When I miscarried, all the precious
names fell from the stars that we
had wished upon. The baby
was gone, and we no longer

remembered those names or the birthday.
Out of my chest, where a heart beat slowly,
a door opened, and tranquility fled
in tiny baby thoughts.

Restless again and thin, I wanted to run,
yet the memory in my womb
reminded me of small fingers and toes.
Until, a year later, the urge to sit in a slow

rocking chair overwhelmed me once again,
and new names returned to dance
their nine-month jig.

Wild Thoughts

They come to me as if in a dream,
those wild thoughts that link brain
to body, to metal loops that adorn
nostrils and navels, a fabrication
to explain my beliefs.

A sleeve in red, green, and blue,
a story told in lines so foreign
and delicate they slant and curl
an artful response to this life.
He sees only a blemish, a flaw
on my skin.

A strong breeze sways the branches
on the tree of his knowledge, the leaves
a void, an ignorance so complete
they repel light for the one who refuses
to see.

Golden Maple

A dry autumn breeze
plays in the branches
of our golden maple.

I gaze to the east and pray
for rain, a light, restorative
smattering.

I watch the silhouette of trees
billowing above
our rooftop

while morning light paints
the sky peach and cream,
a revelation.

Hara

She worked the
flanges of my
inner hip,
       the hara,
       the hard bone
       surrounding, soft flesh.

She stirred the stew
of my belly bowl,
released the ache
       I'd collected during days
       of carrying boxes filled
       with memories, covered in dust.

I traveled those boxes
like a breeze blown through
A broken window,
       the sharp glass
       slicing the flow.

I came to her ancient
and at one with my pain.
She pulled the bowl
       of my belly
       inside out, and I

       glistened once more.

ADDITIONAL ACKNOWLEDGMENTS

I would like to thank Deborah Woodard for her constant support in all things poetry and for her friendship that transcends poetry. Marjorie Rommel for her inspiration. Trevor O'Hara for his keen eye and ability in the craft. And last but not least, the Black Diamond Crew, Ardi, Harvey, Suzanne, and Skeeter, who always let me know when something is working and when it isn't. My poetry is better for their valuable critiques.

Avis Adams was born and raised in the Puget Sound area of Washington. Many of her poems have won awards and found homes in print and in online journals. This is her first book of poetry. She has a Masters in English Literature and teaches at Green River College. When she isn't writing or teaching, she's hiking, cross-country skiing, gardening, doing photography. She also loves to travel the world with her husband, visit her two grown children, and walk her dog.

www.ingramcontent.com/pod-product-compliance
Lightning Source LLC
LaVergne TN
LVHW041557070426
835507LV00011B/1129